Coloring Our World

To order additional copies of this book, contact:
Xlibris Corporation
1-888-795-4274
www.Xlibris.com
Orders@Xlibris.com
66229

It is realistic, we live in a multicultural society. This coloring book provides an awareness with a special message of unity, while identifying different cultures, the integration of the drawings and the activities.

The genuine purpose of this booklet is dedicated to the appreciation and development of a sense of pride for all cultures, and the creation of unity and individual self-esteem.

Alberta Adams

This booklet has been possible through a grant from:

AETNA Life & Casualty

A Graduate Student Project 1990

by Alberta Adams

A Comprehensive Child Development Programs
was implemented consisting of key components to ensure that
Head Start programs provide the services necessary
to meet the goals of these components

Education
Head Start's
educational
program is
designed to
meet each
child's
individual
need of the
community
served and its
ethic and
cultural
characteristics.

My Friends Come To Visit Me

MY FRIENDS COME TO PLAY WITH ME

BLACK
AMERICAN

NATIVE
AMERICAN

AMERICAN
LATIN AMERICAN

__Health__— Head Start emphasizes the importance of Early identification of health problems. Head Start provides every child with an A-1 comprehensive health care program, including medical, dental, mental health & nutritional services.

WE ENJOY NATURE TOGETHER

ASIAN AMERICAN

LATIN AMERICAN

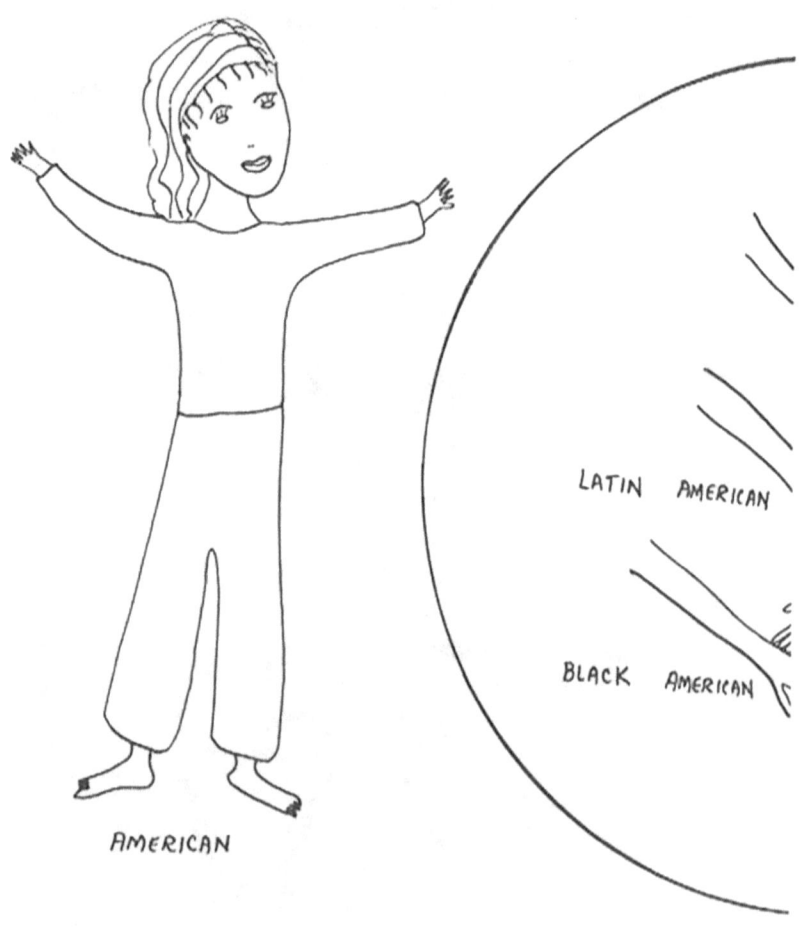

Monhandas K. Gandhi

TOGETHER WE

Jesse Jackson

LATIN AMERICAN

BLACK AMERICAN

AMERICAN

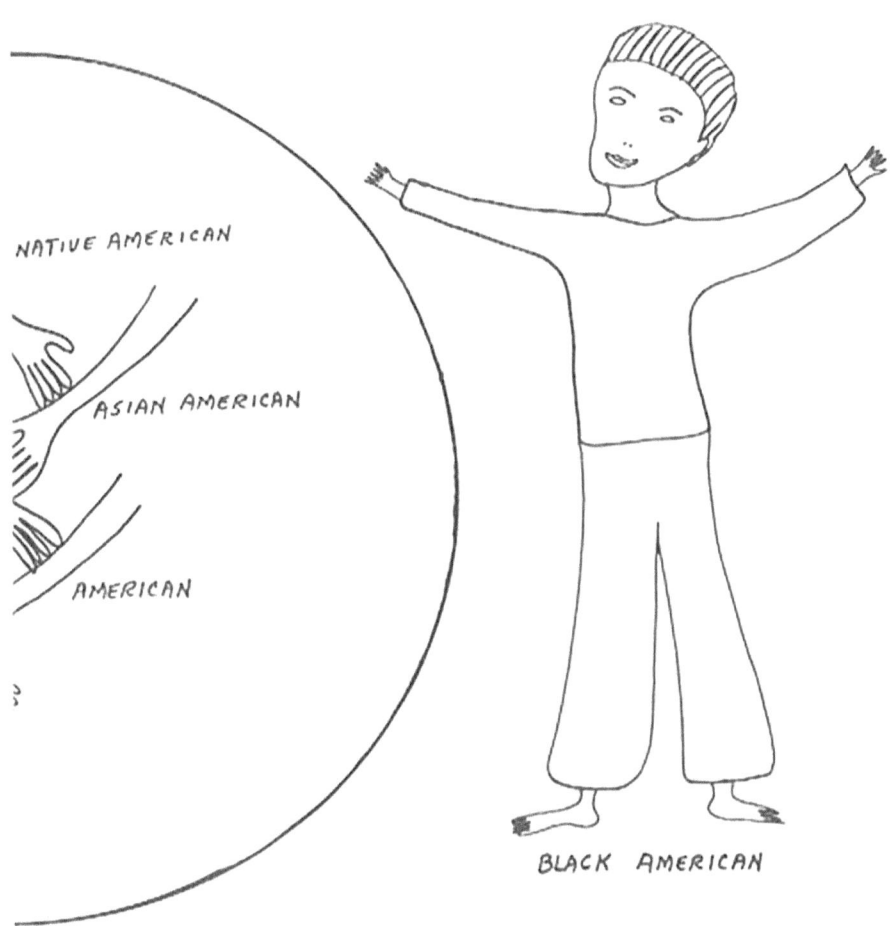

MAKE OUR WORLD

John F. Kennedy

Martin Luther King, Jr.

NATIVE AMERICAN

ASIAN AMERICAN

AMERICAN

BLACK AMERICAN

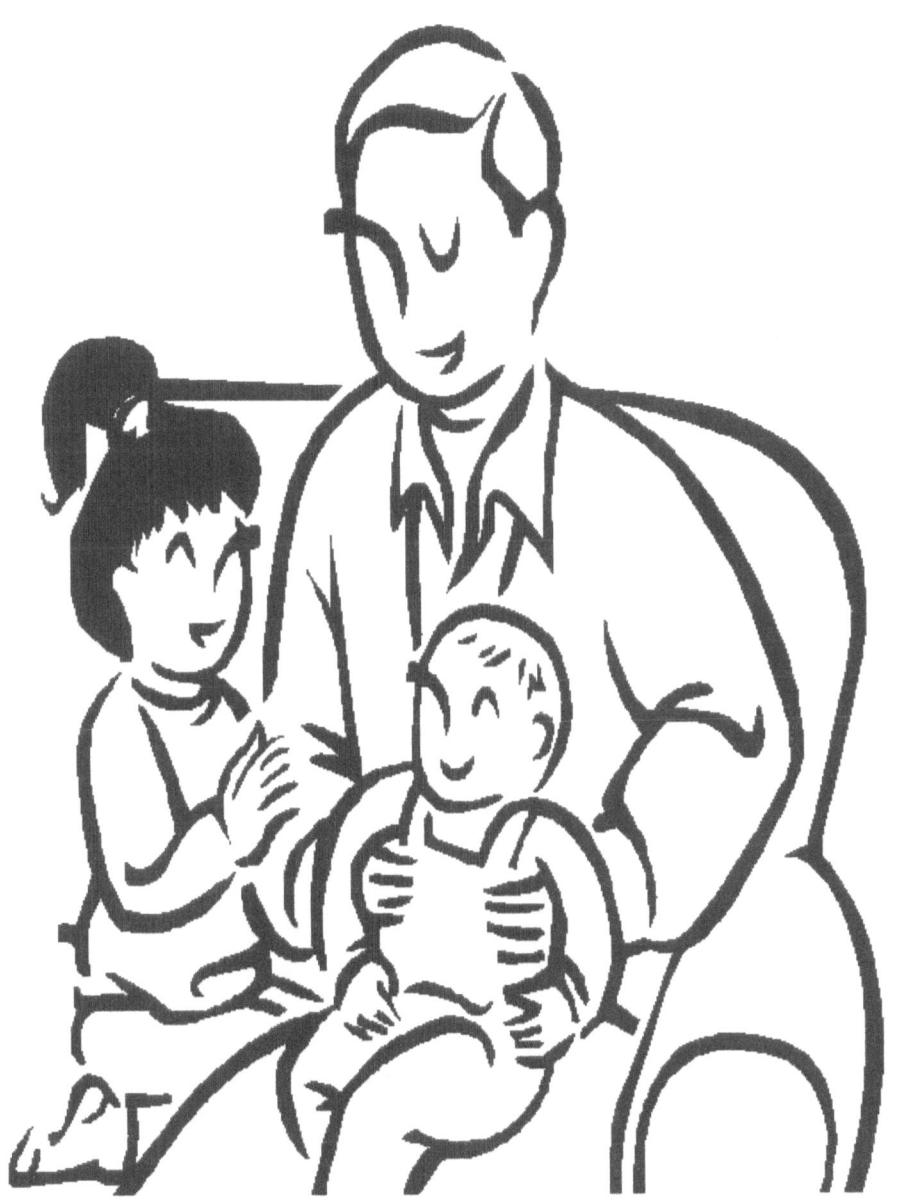

Parent Involvement-
Parents are the most important influence on a child's development.
An essential part of every Head Start program is the involvement
of the parents in parent education, pro-parent involvement in the
program, and assistance to parents in overcoming economic and
personal problems

Staff Development & Training

The Head Start program provides staff at all levels and in all program areas with training to improve job performance and opportunities for career advancement with the program. The Child Development Associate (CDA) Program gives professional and nonprofessional employees the opportunity to study child development.

WE SING TOGETHER IN HARMONY

BLACK
AMERICAN

AMERICAN

ASIAN
AMERICAN

LATIN
AMERICAN

He Made Them All

All things bright and beautiful,
all creatures great and small,
and all things wise and wonderful,
He made them all.

Each little flower that opens,
each little bird that sings,
He made their glowing odors,
He made their tiny wings.

The purple-headed mountain,
the river running by the sunset,
and the morning that brightens up the sky.
The cold wind in the winter,
the pleasant summer sun,
The ripe fruits in the garden,

He made them every one

By Cecil F. Alexander, 1823-1895

What lies behind us
and what lies before us
are small matters
compared to what lies
within us.

Ralph Waldo Emerson

A Child Development Program
U.S. Department of Health & Human Services

In 1969, Head Start
was delegated from
The Office of Economic Opportunity
to The Office of Child Development in
The U.S. Department of Health,
Education & Welfare,
and has now become a program
within
The Administration of Children,
Youth & Families at
The Department of Health &
Human Services.

Coloring Our World

The purpose of the booklet is to bring awareness of equality & justice for all people & begin to educate children at a young age in a very simplistic manner. Usage of this booklet will be a tool for educational purposes, discussions to young children & others who may take interest in learning about multicultural & how people can do things together as the coloring of descriptive figures are realized.

The many cultures in our society & their interactions, reflects how togetherness & equality for all people can exist. The booklet is an expression of concerns that reveals an individual interpretation & conveys an education to youngster and how to embrace equality for all people.

Helen Hayes said, and I quote, "My mother drew a distinction between achievement and success. She said that achievement is the knowledge that you have studied and worked hard and done the best that is in you. Success is being praised by others, and that is nice, too, but not as important or satisfying. Always aim for achievement and forget about success." I'm a woman of color, 45 years of age, living in a suburban community. This experience was overwhelming, but more importantly rewarding. It enhanced my knowledge and awareness of the existence of barriers that are yet prevalent in our society today.
"Someday perhaps change will occur when times are ready for it instead of always when it is too late. Someday change will be accepted as life itself."
Shirley MacLaine

In Preparation for this booklet, I referenced a collection of books, visited daycares, preschool programs, early childhood centers, conducted interviews, consulted with staff and canvassed parents to ensure that the contents were adequate and appropriate for youngsters. Also, I visited several libraries researching books, posters and other educational aide that illustrated information youngsters could relate to.

Regional Offices Location of the
Offices of Human Development Services
Department of Health & Human Services

Region 1
Government Center
Federal Building Rm 2000
Boston, MA, 02203
(617) 233-6450

Region 2
26 Federal Plaza
Federal Building Rm 4149
New York, NY, 10007
(212)264-3472

Region 3
3535 Market St.
(PO Box 13716)
Philadelphia, PA, 19101
(215) 596-0356

Region 4
101 Marietta Tower Suite 903
Atlanta, GA, 30323
(404) 242-2134

Region 5
300 South Wacker Dr. 13th Flr
Chicago, IL, 60606
(312) 353-8322

Region 6
1200 Main Tower Building
Dallas, TX, 75202
(214) 767-2976

Region 7
601 E, 12th Street
Rm 384 Federal Building
Kansas City, MO, 64106
(616) 374-3981

Region 8
1961 Stout Street, Rm 908
Denver, CO, 80294
(803) 844-2622

Region 9
50 United Nations Plaza,
Rm. 455
San Francisco, CA, 94102
(415) 556-4029

Region 10
2901, 3rd Avenue,
3rd & Broad Building,
Seattle, WA, 98121
(206) 442-2430

HUMAN SERVICES
· WE ·
CARE
SPRINGFIELD COLLLEGE

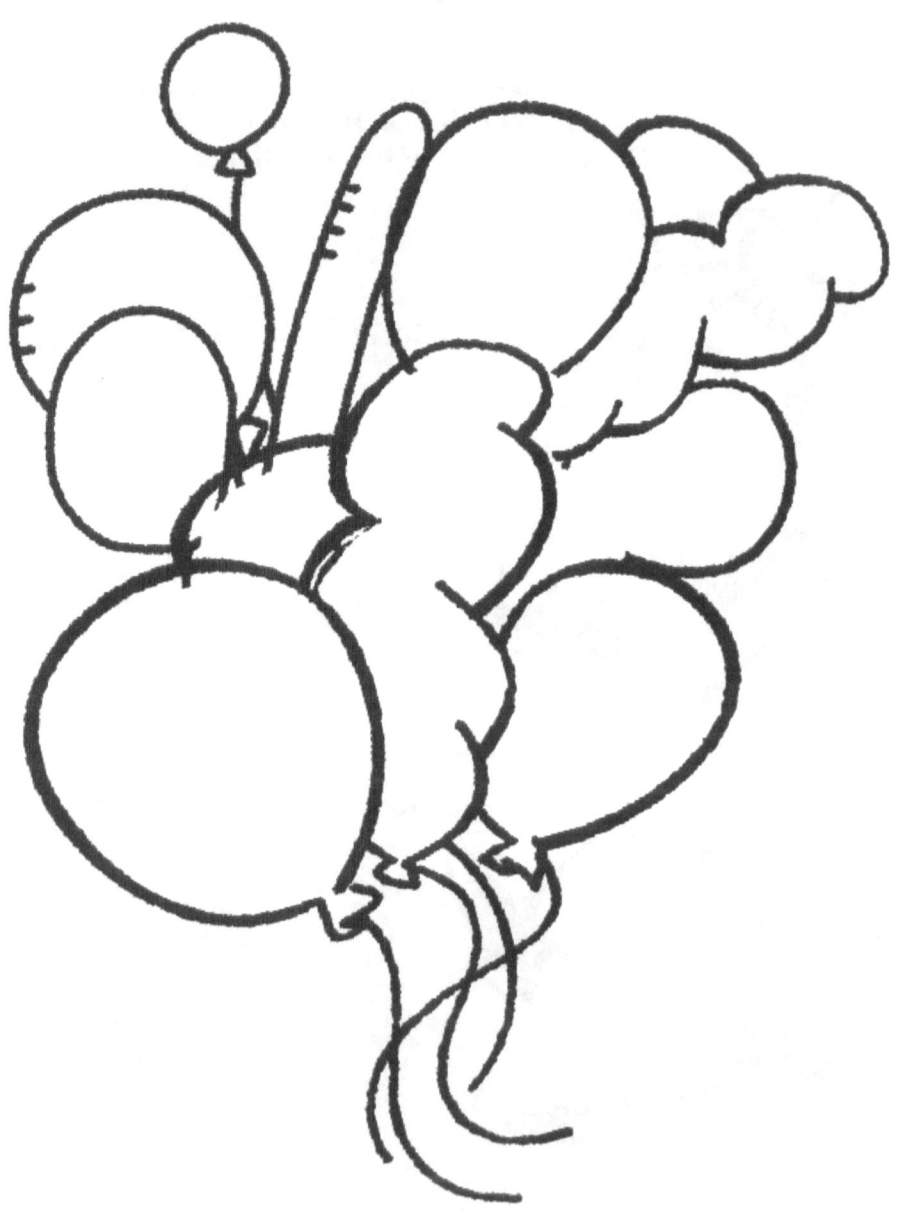